Healing Through Mandala Coloring

Welcome to a world of relaxation and self-exploration with "Mandala Meditation: A Journey in Coloring." This isn't just a coloring book; it's a pathway to tranquility and mental wellness. Mandalas have long been a tool for meditation, offering significant therapeutic benefits, especially for those managing mental health challenges.

Let your intuition guide your choice of colors and designs. There are no rules - just paths to peace and creativity. While beneficial, remember this is a complementary activity to professional mental health care, not a replacement.

Embrace each mandala as a step towards inner calm and emotional resilience.

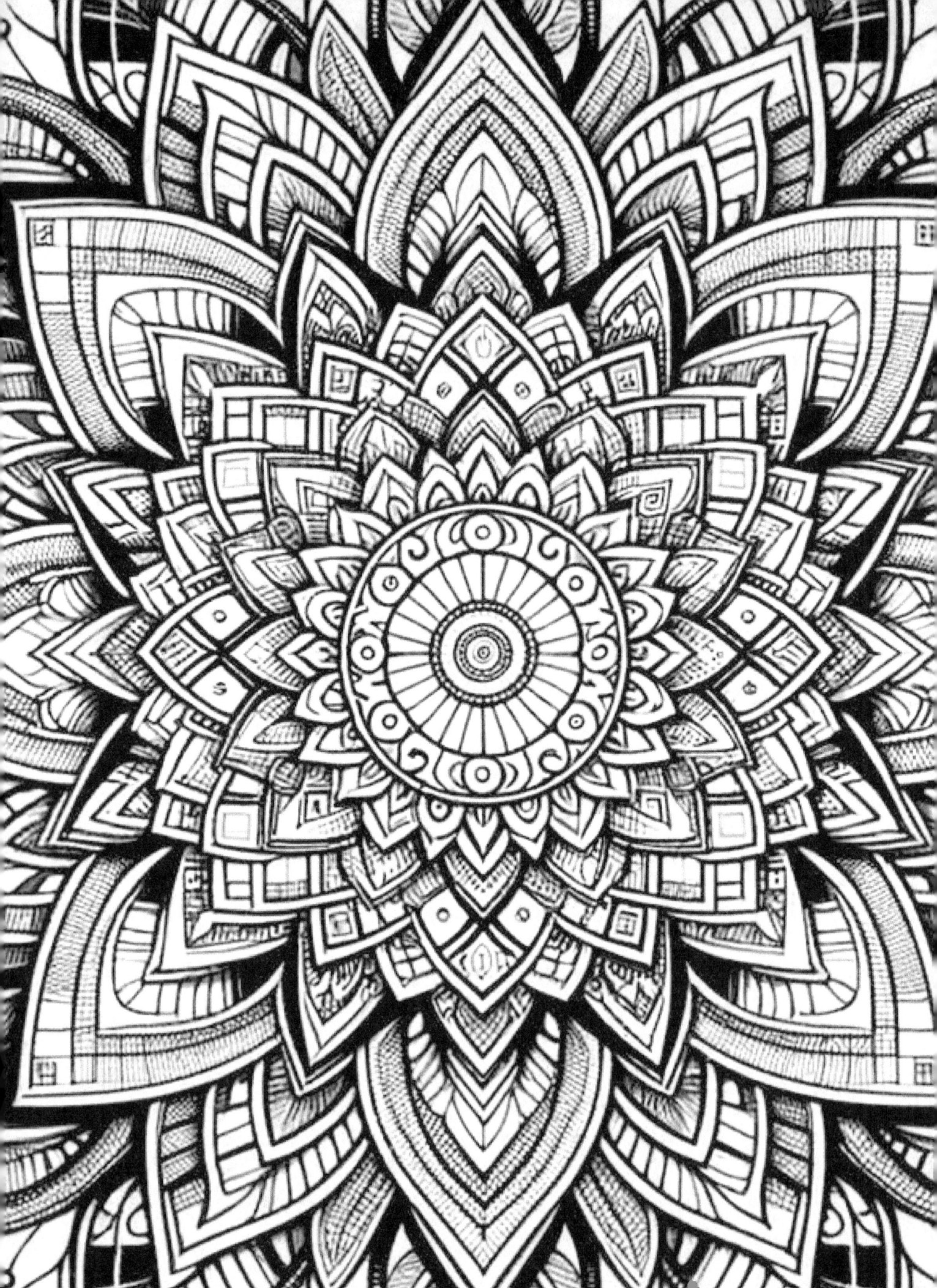

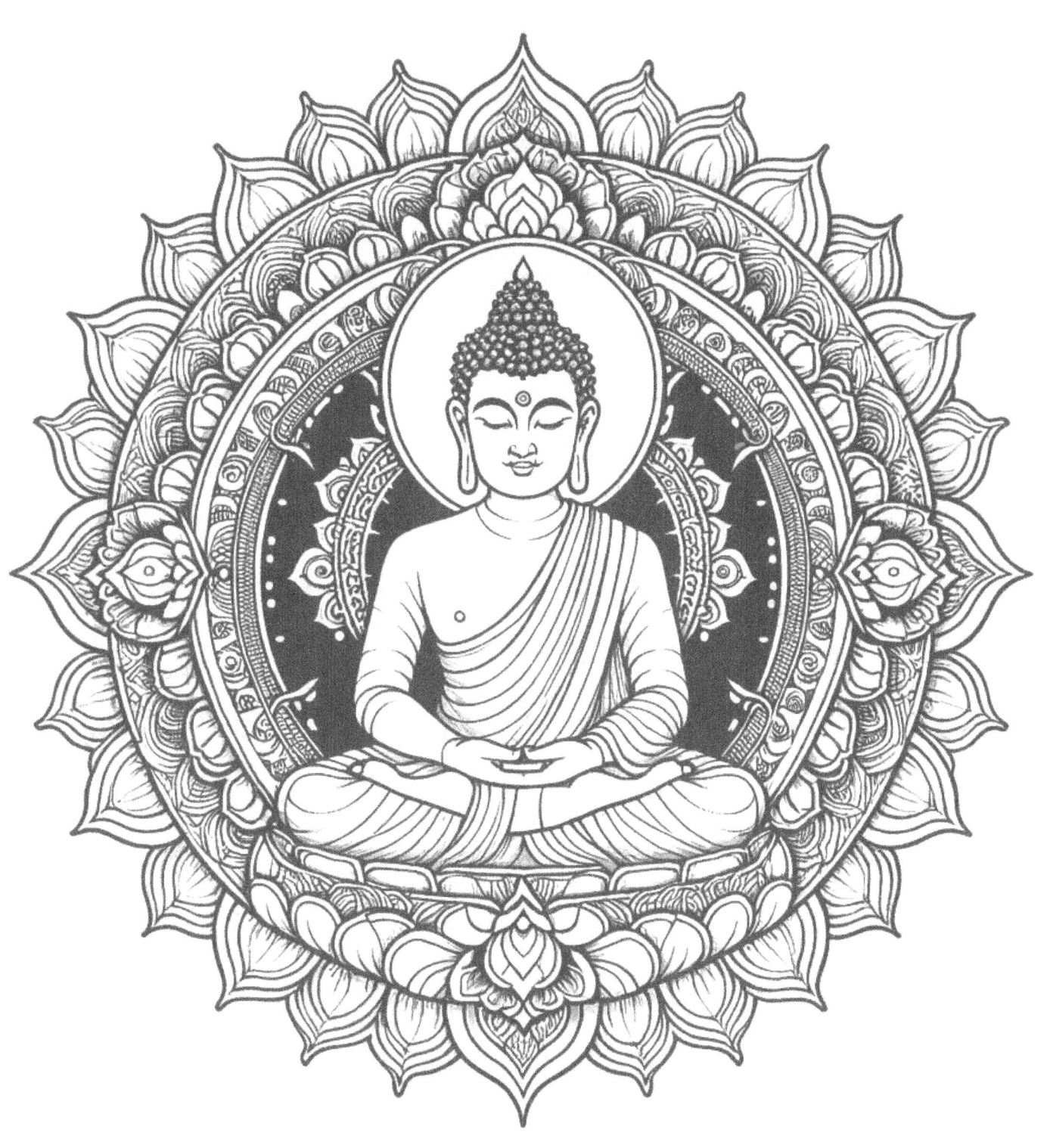

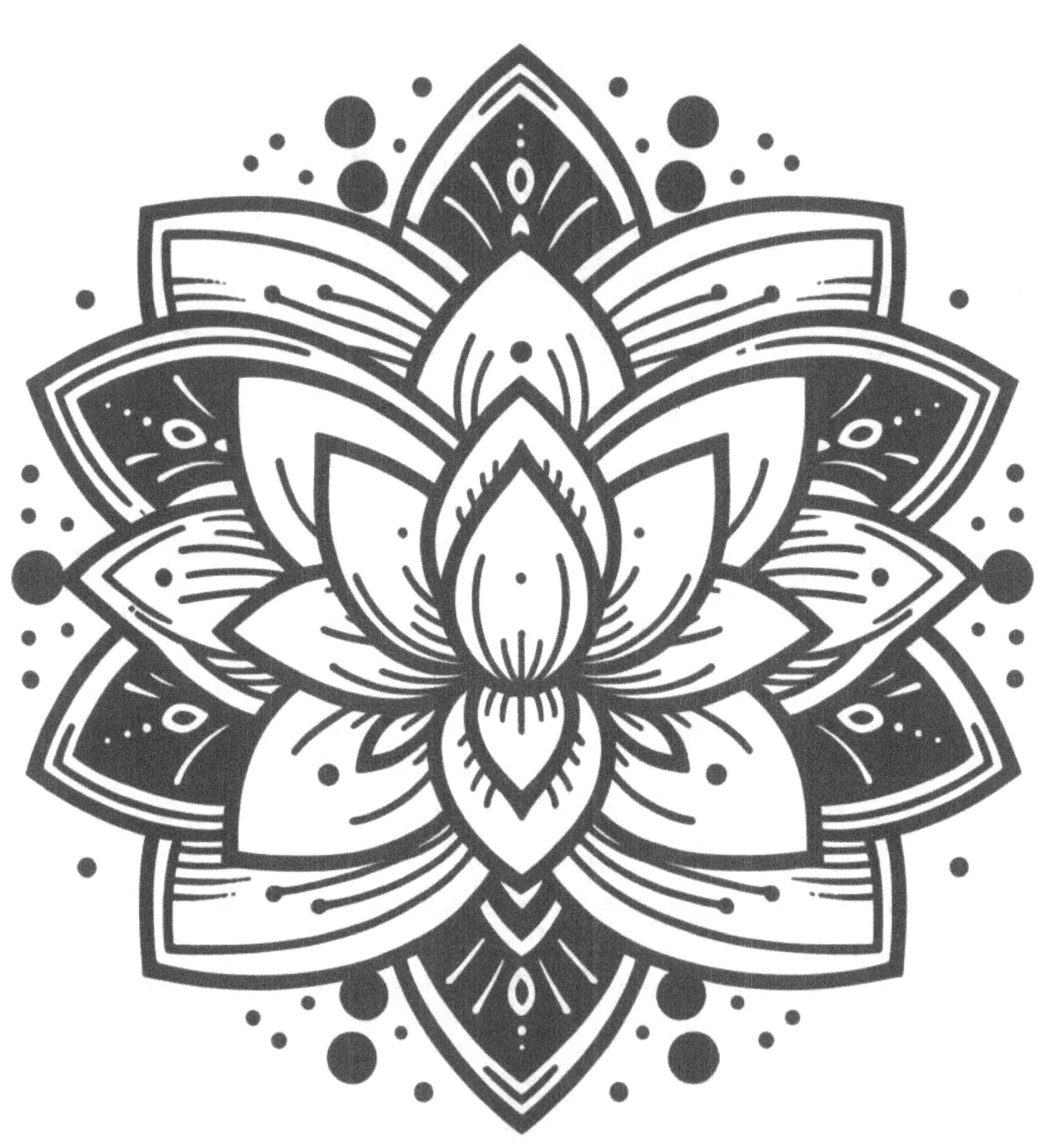

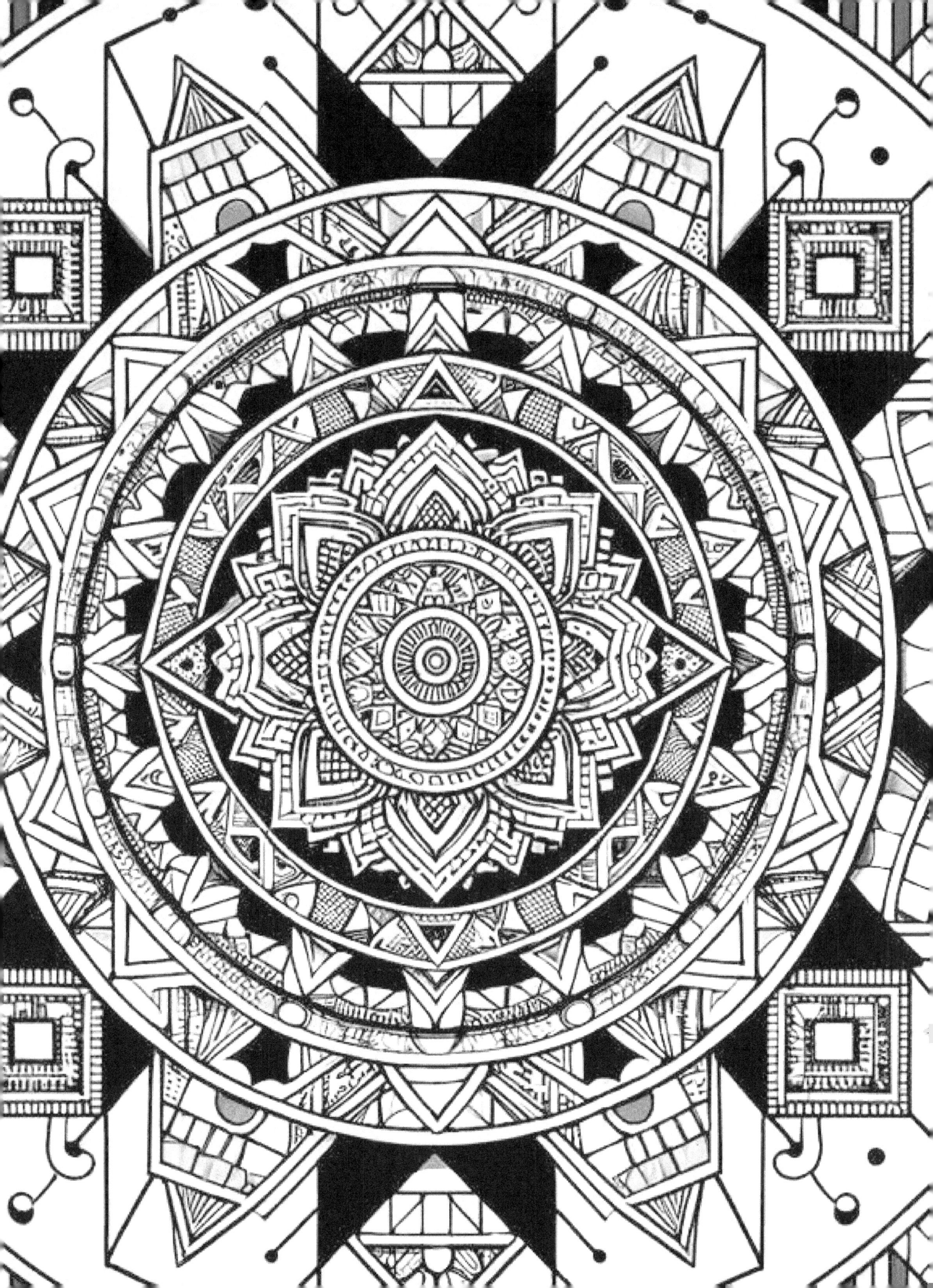

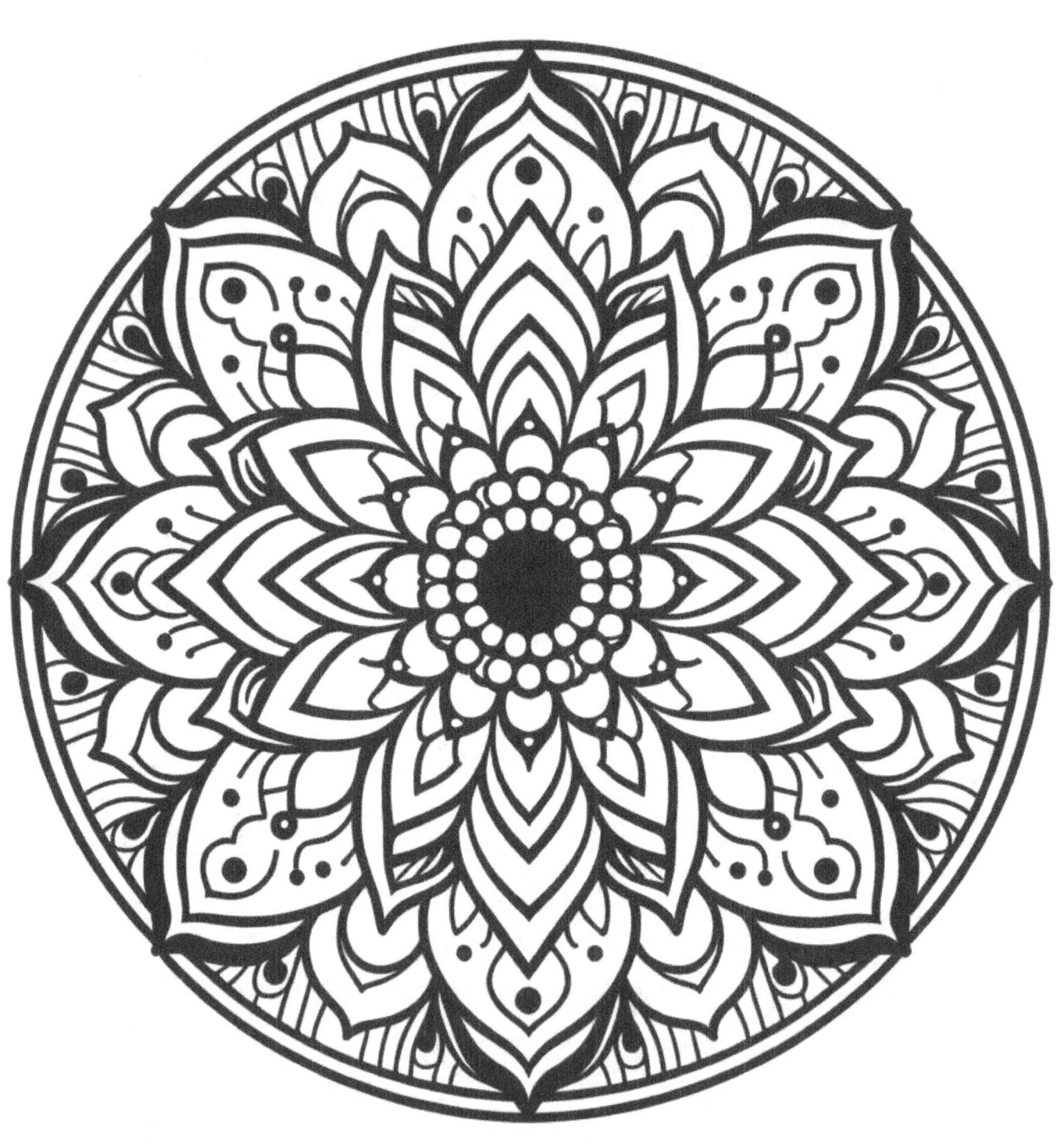

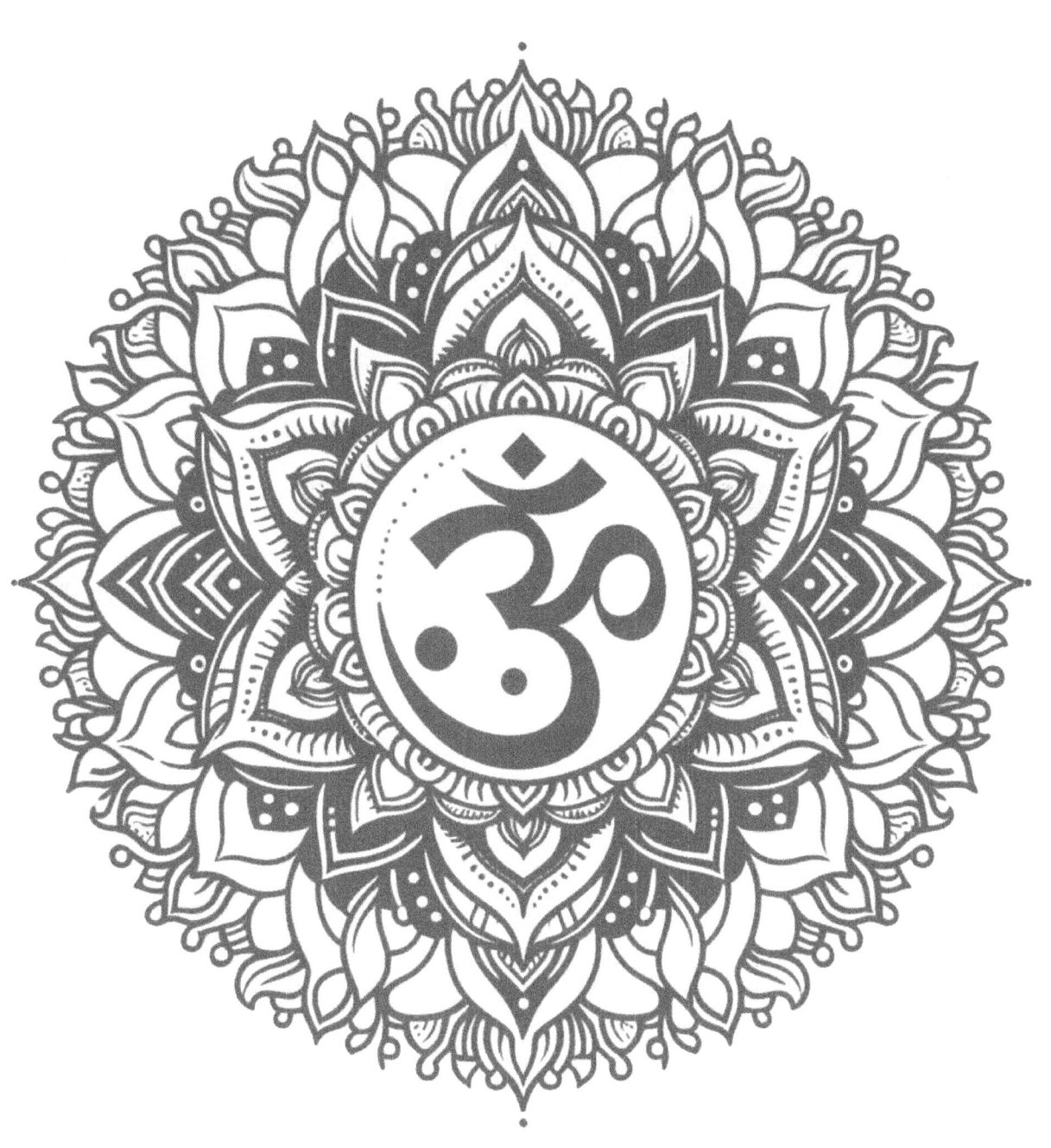

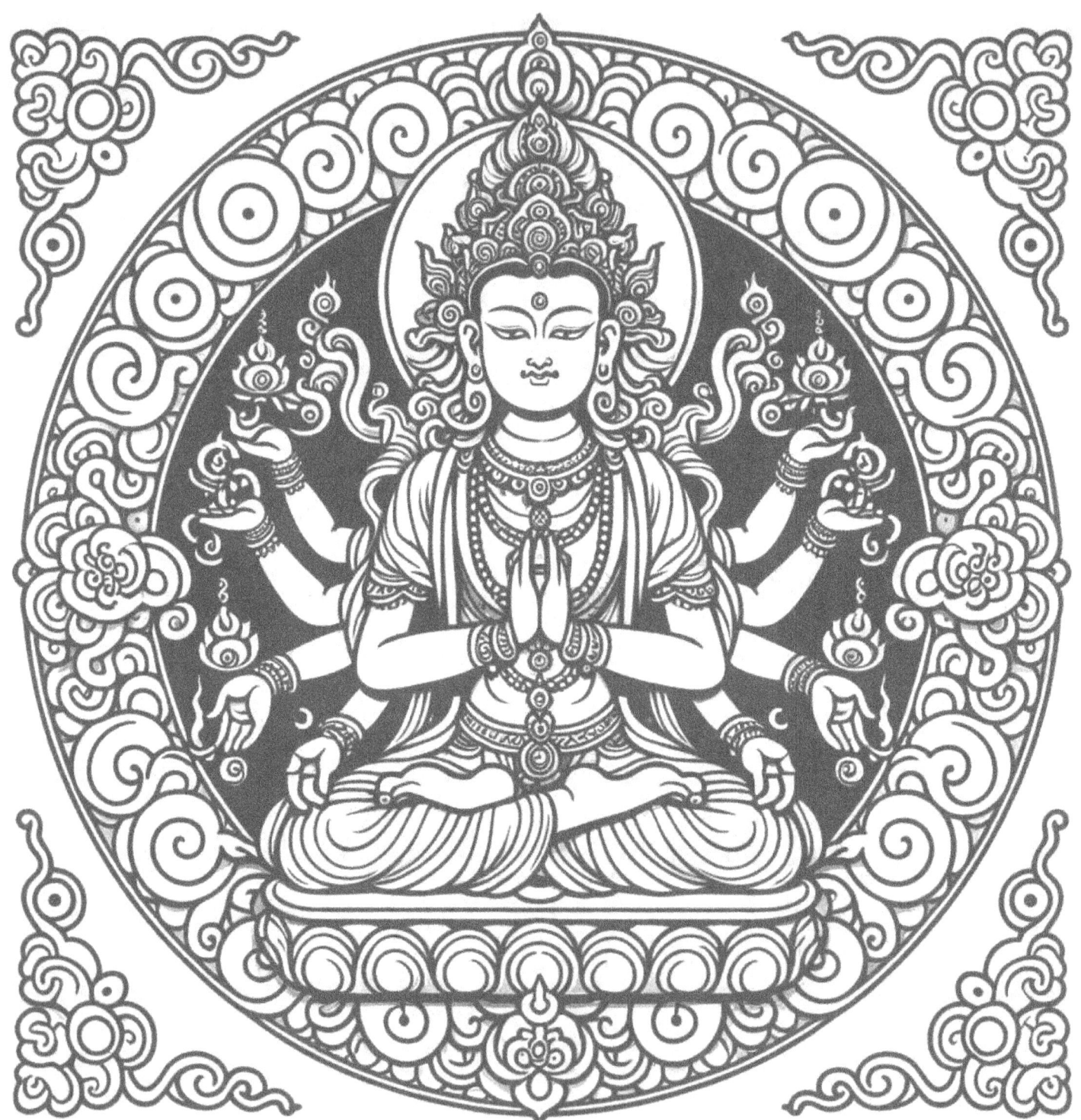

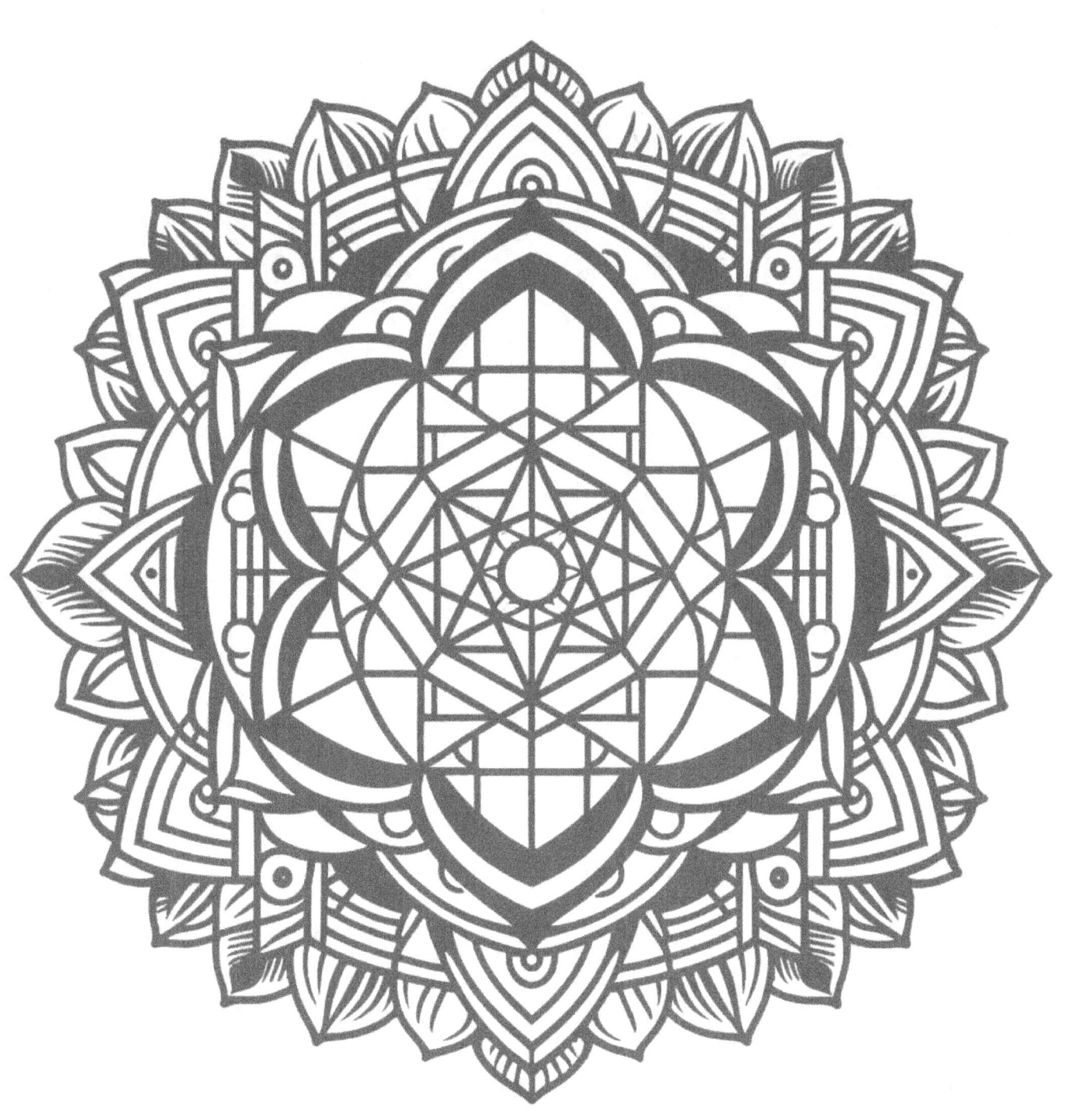

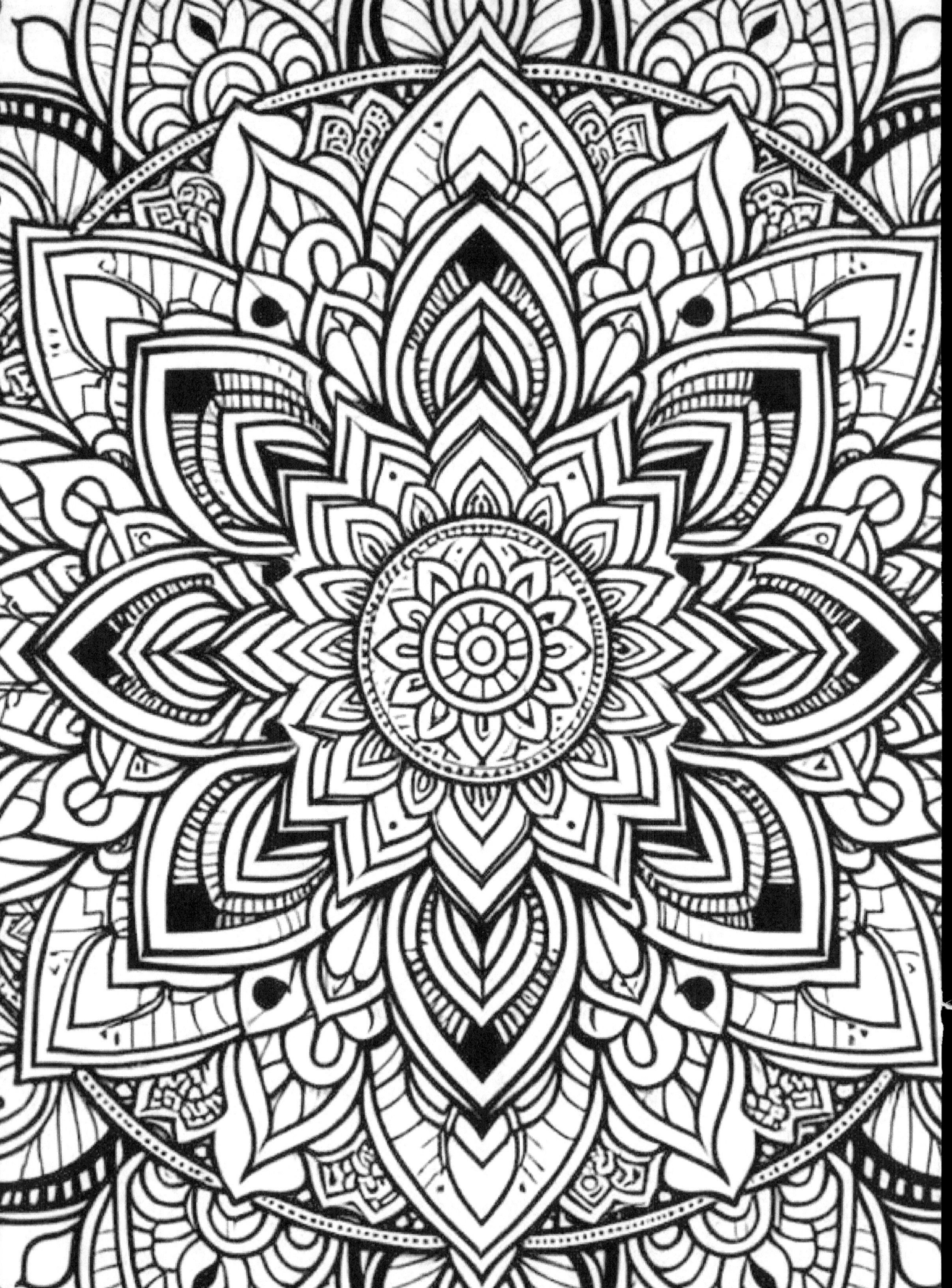

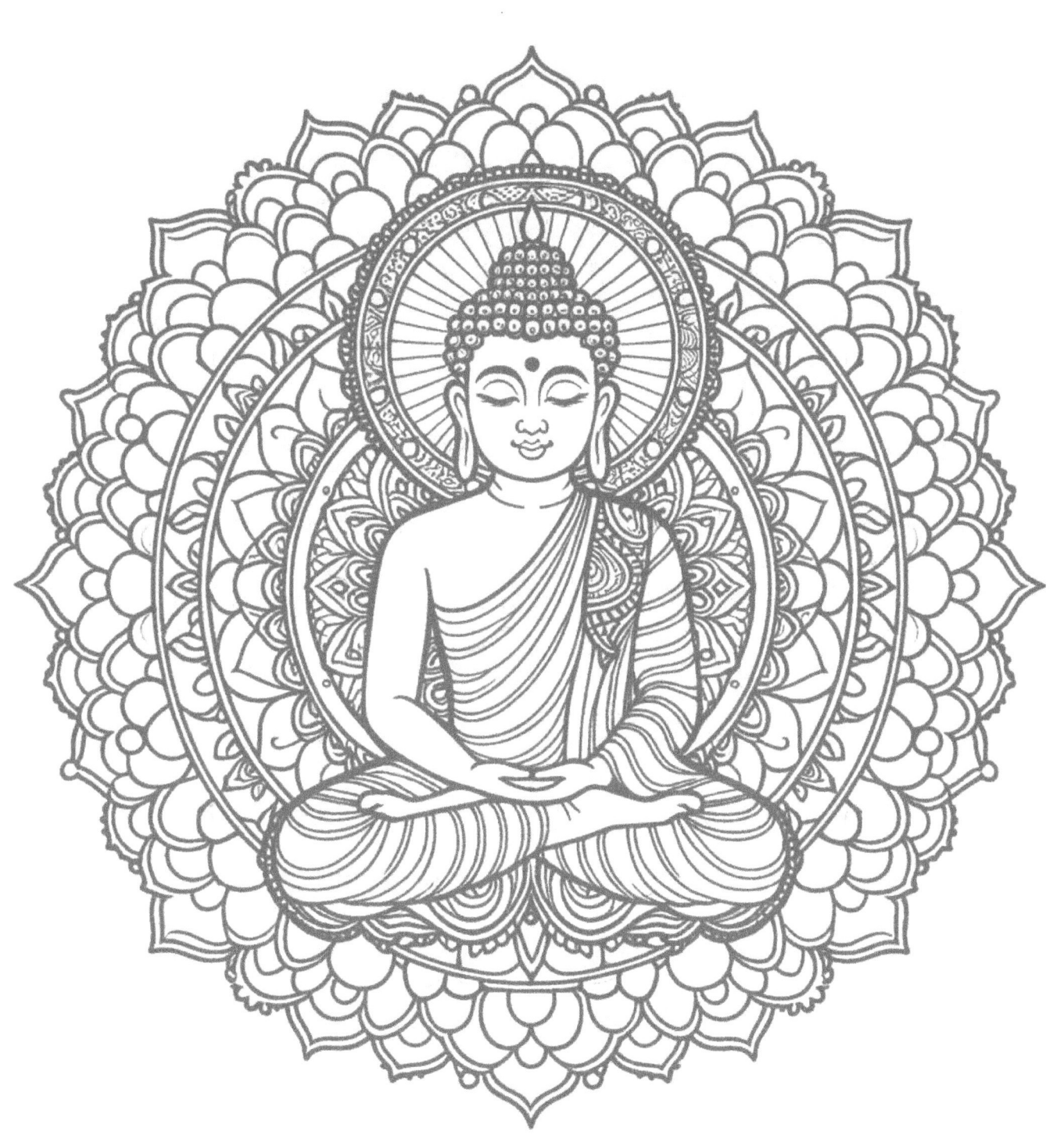

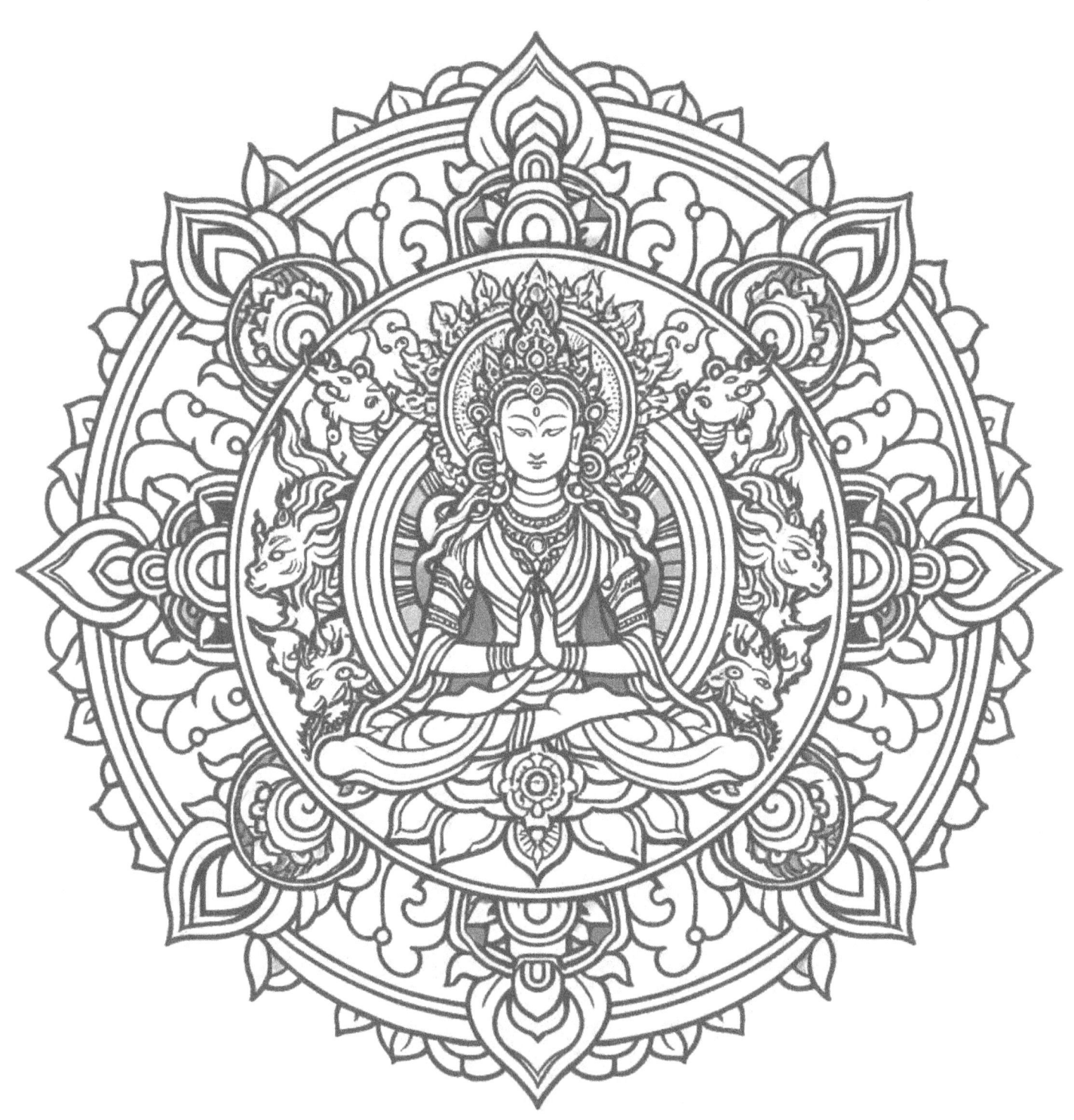

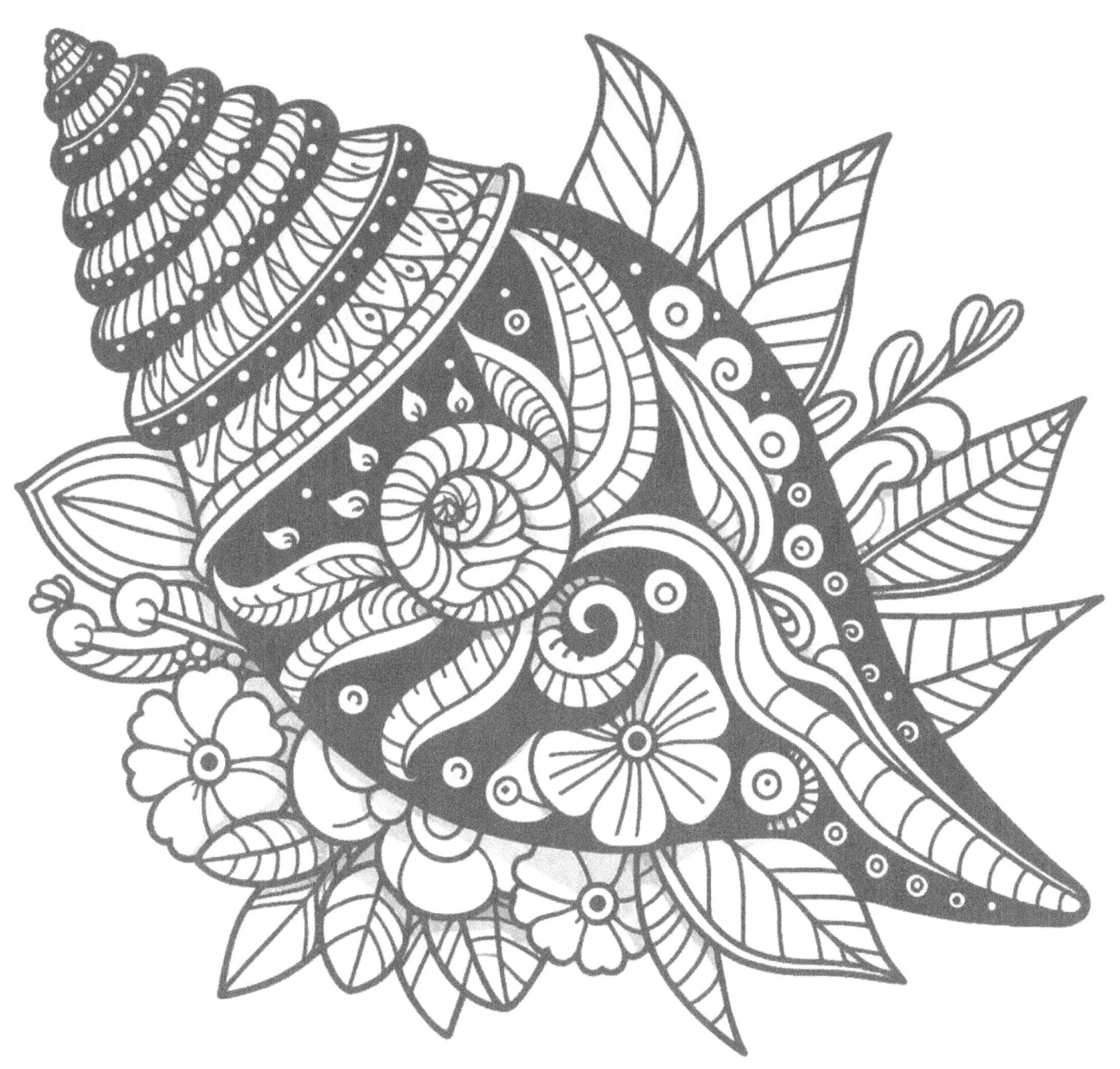

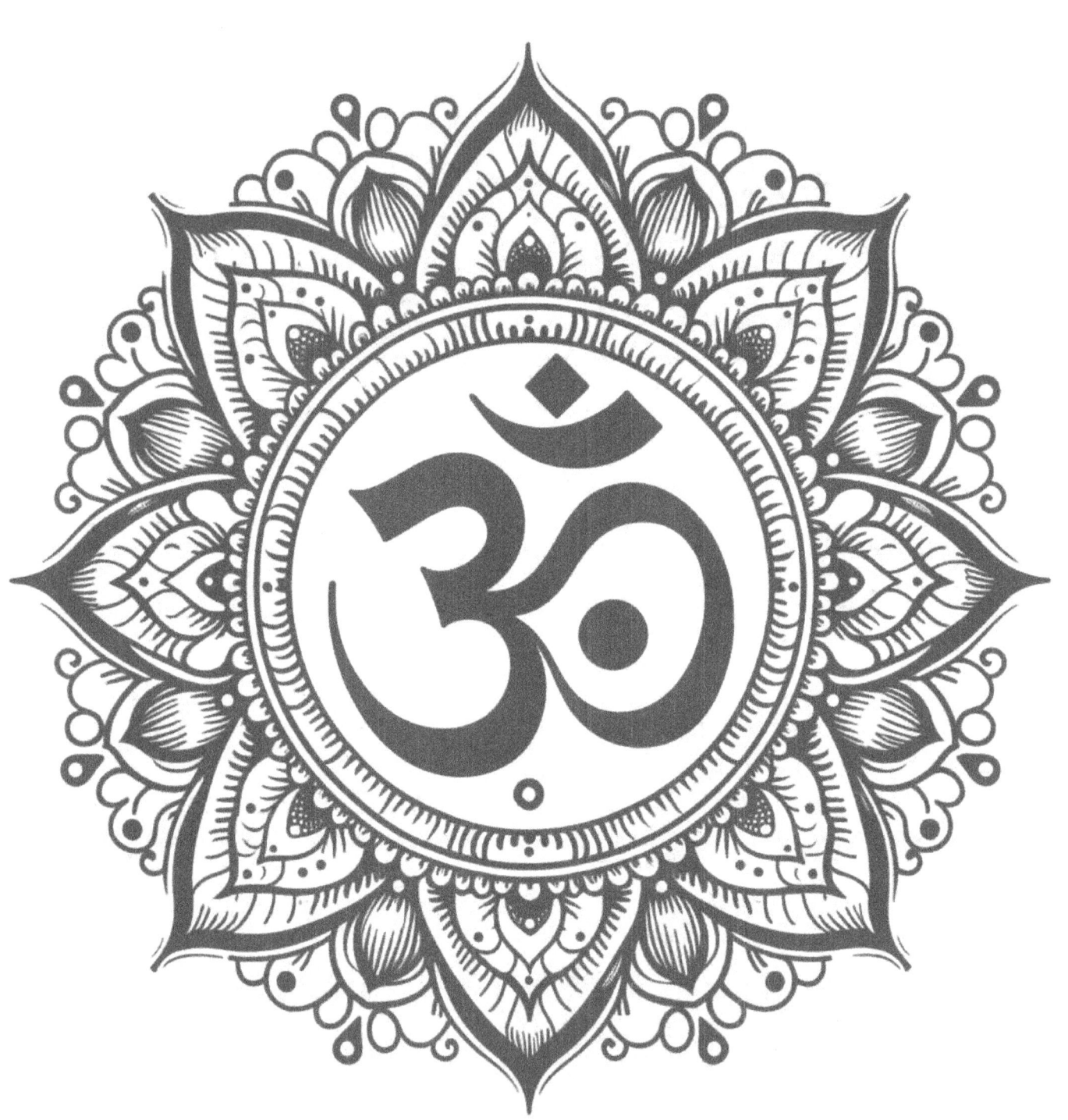

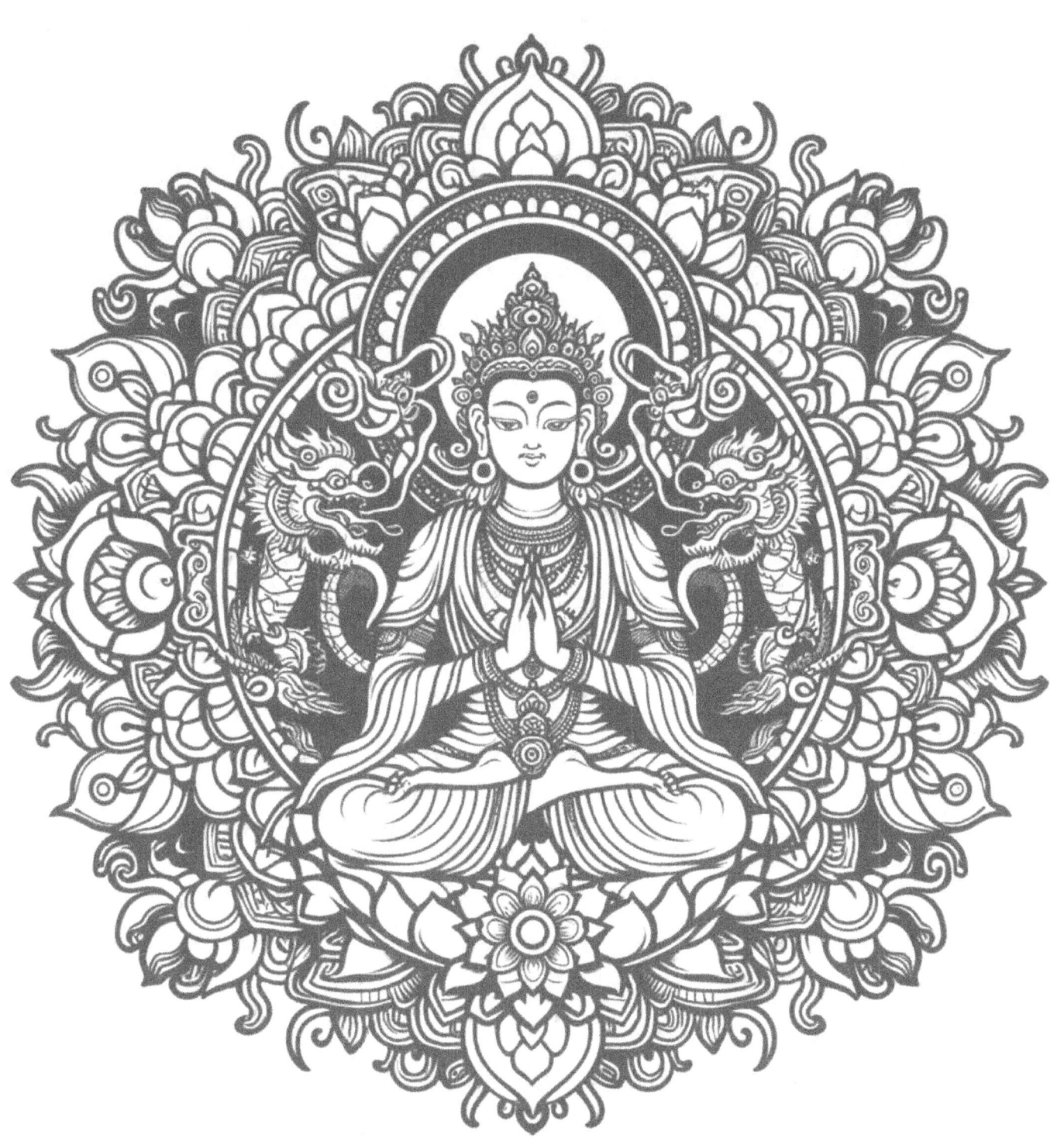

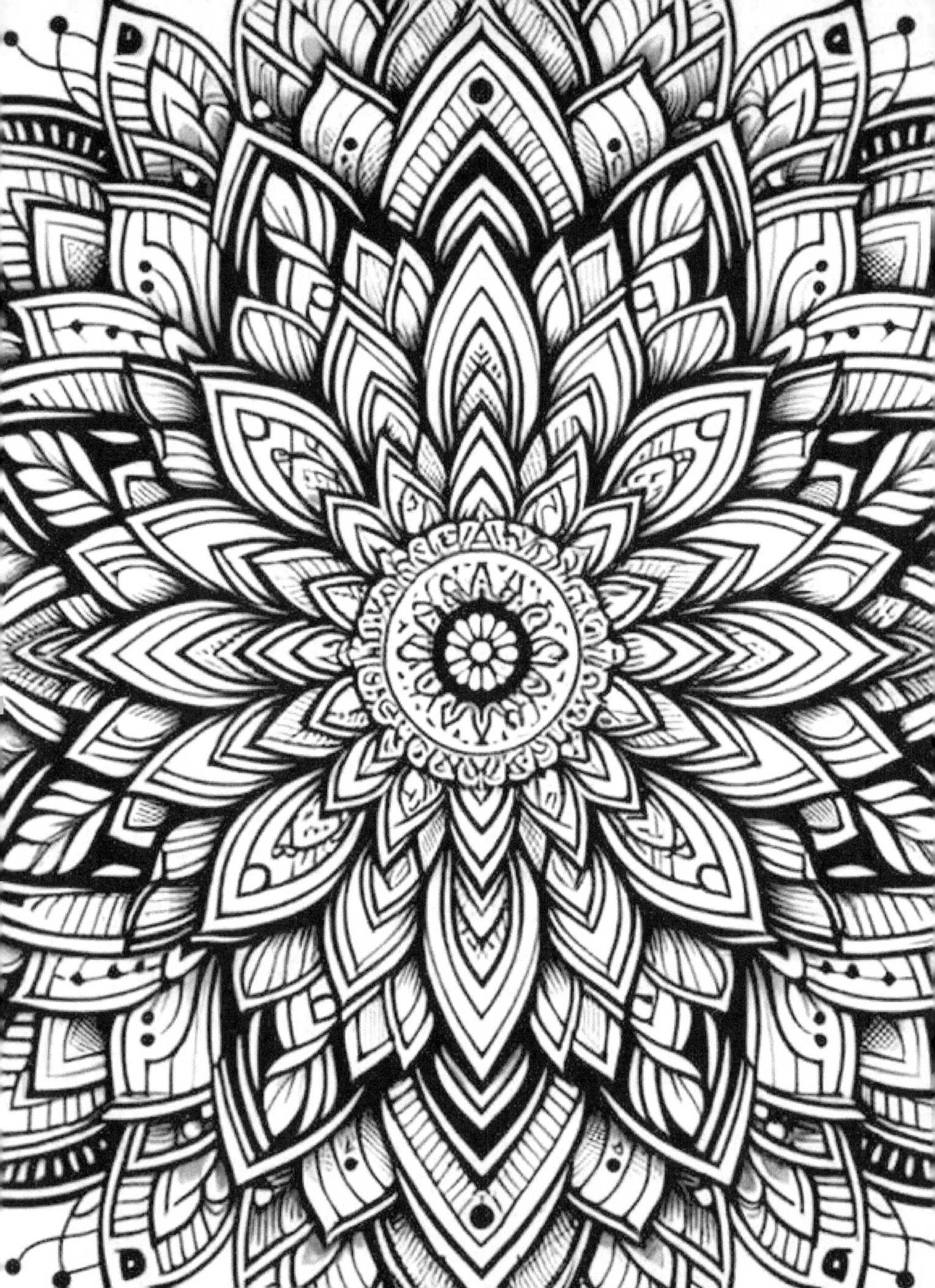

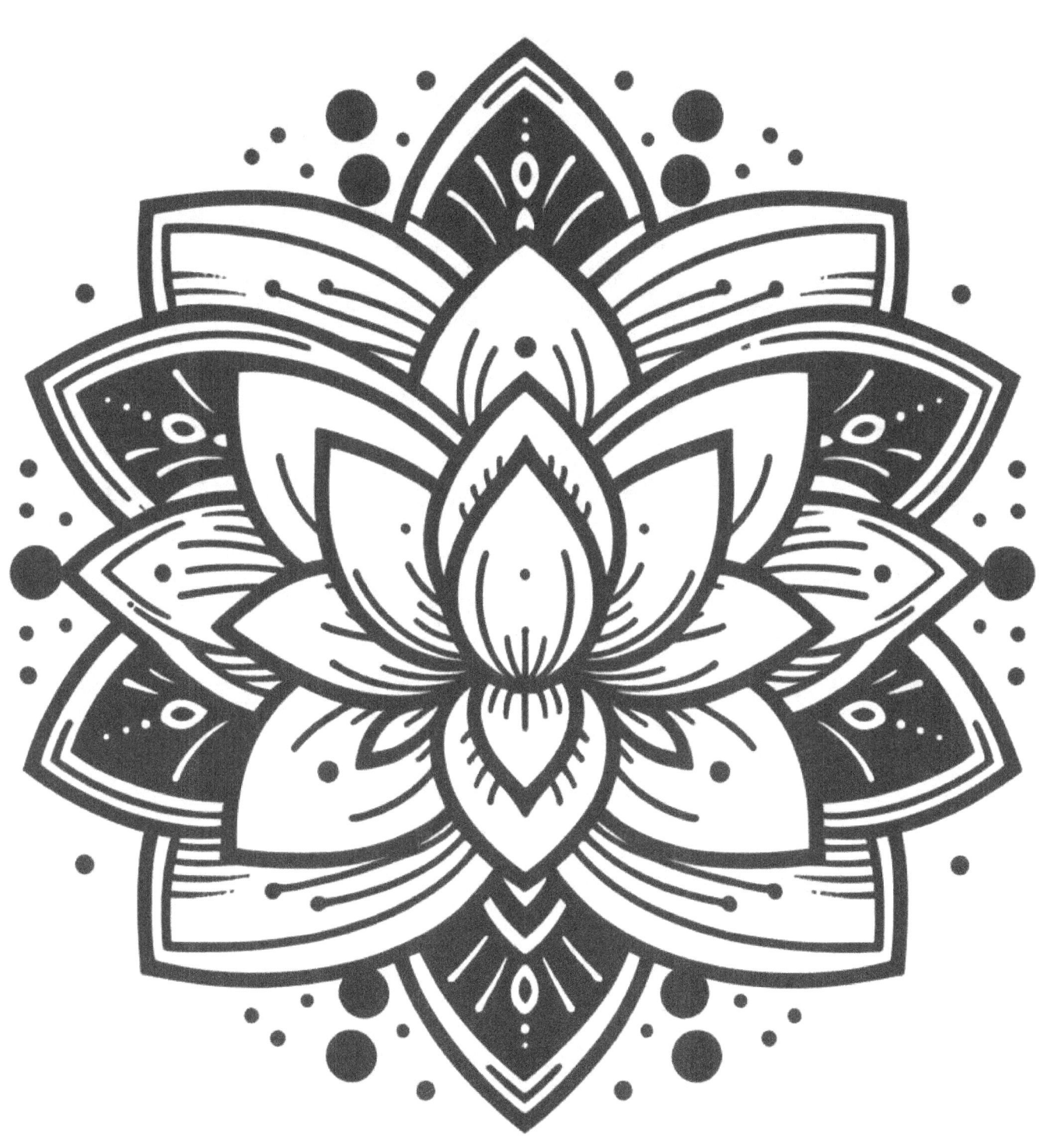

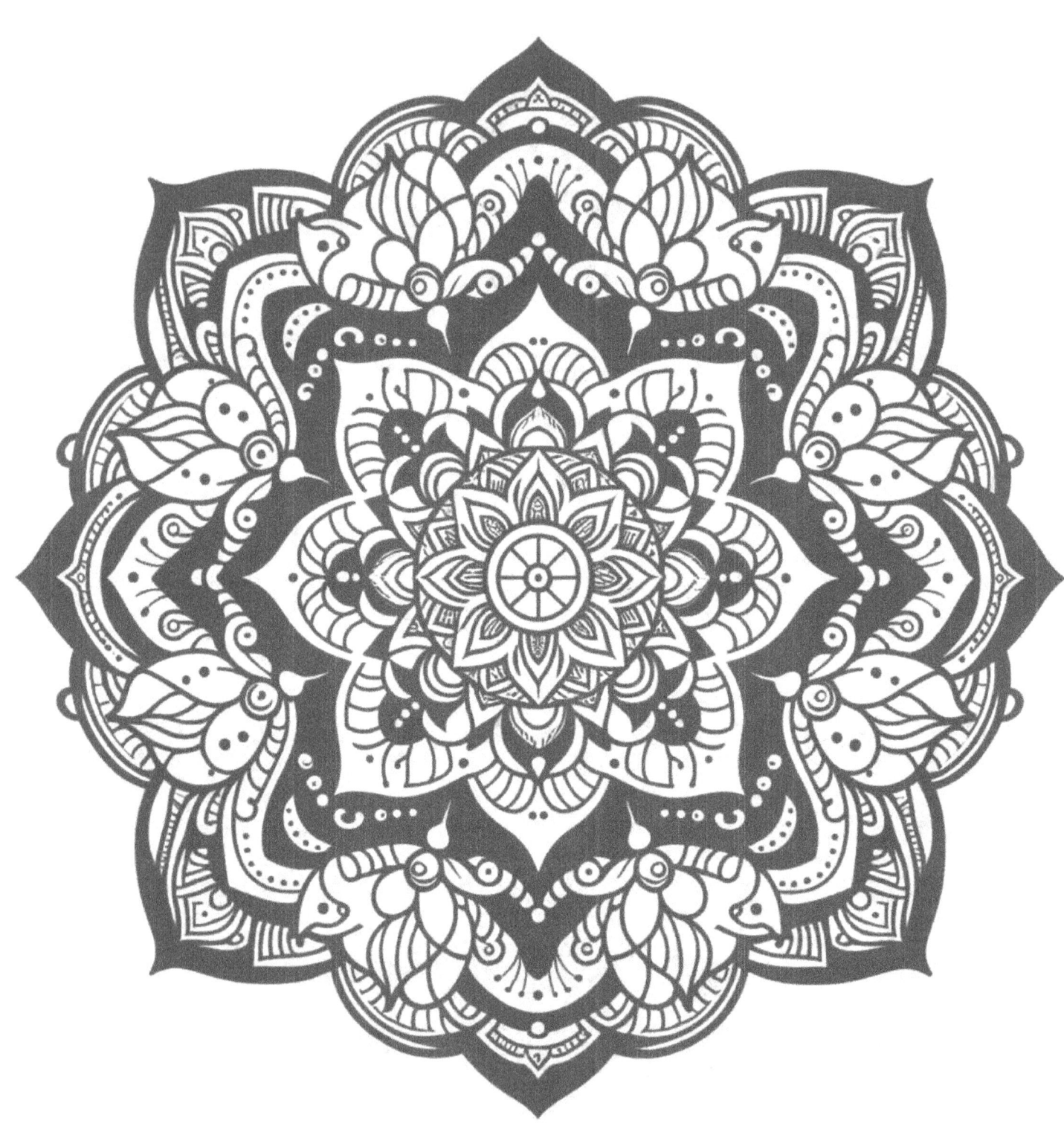

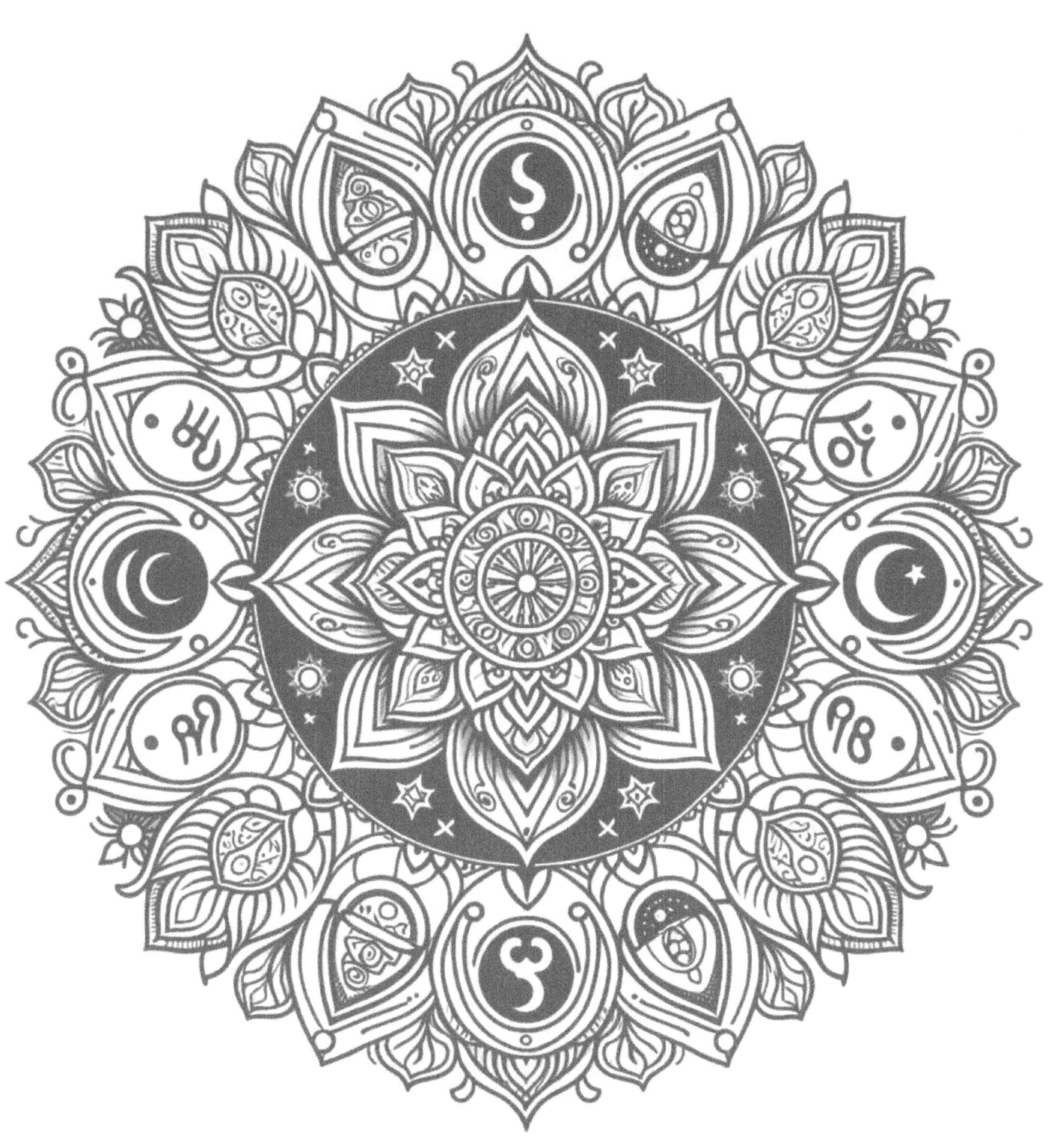

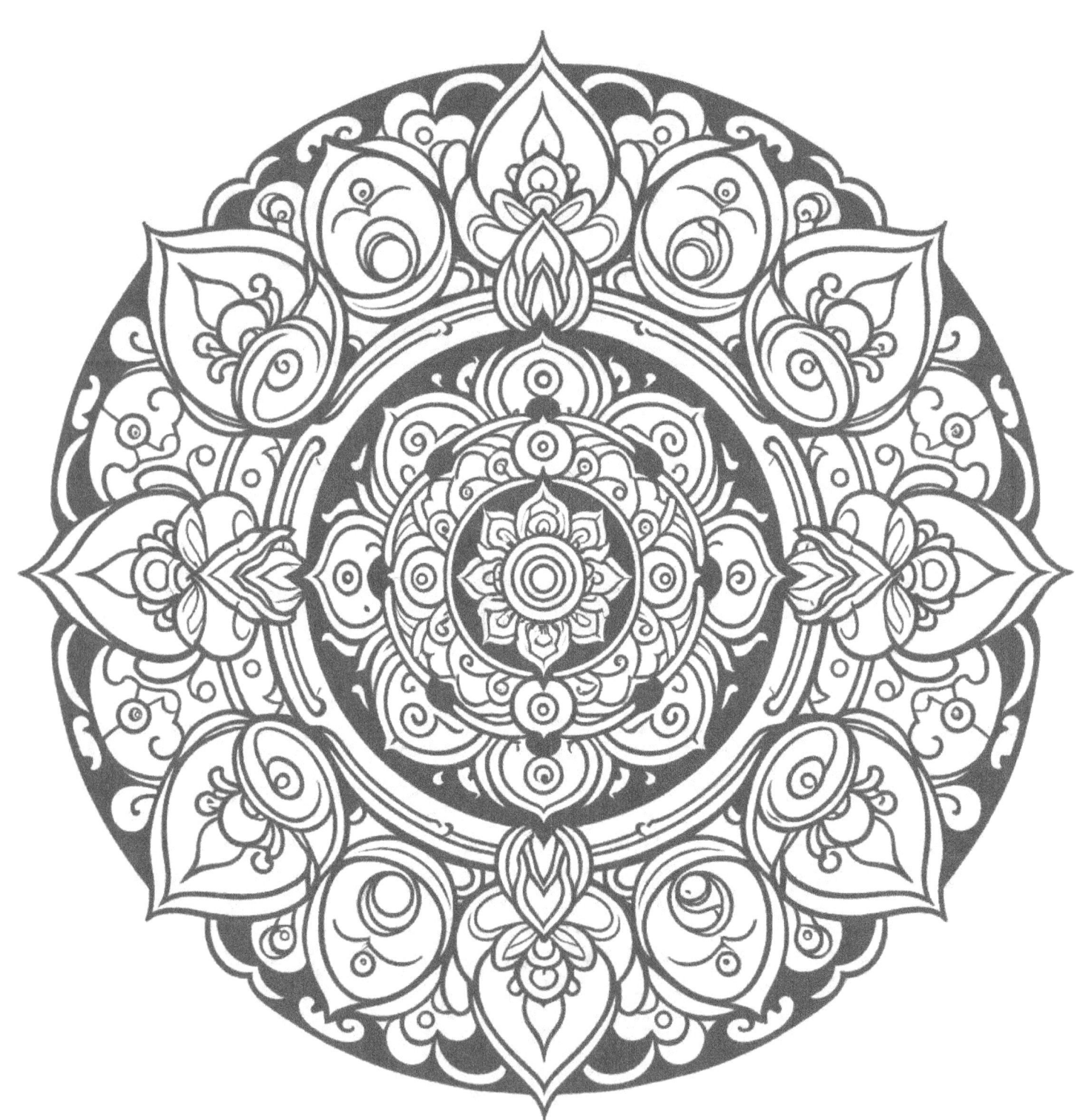

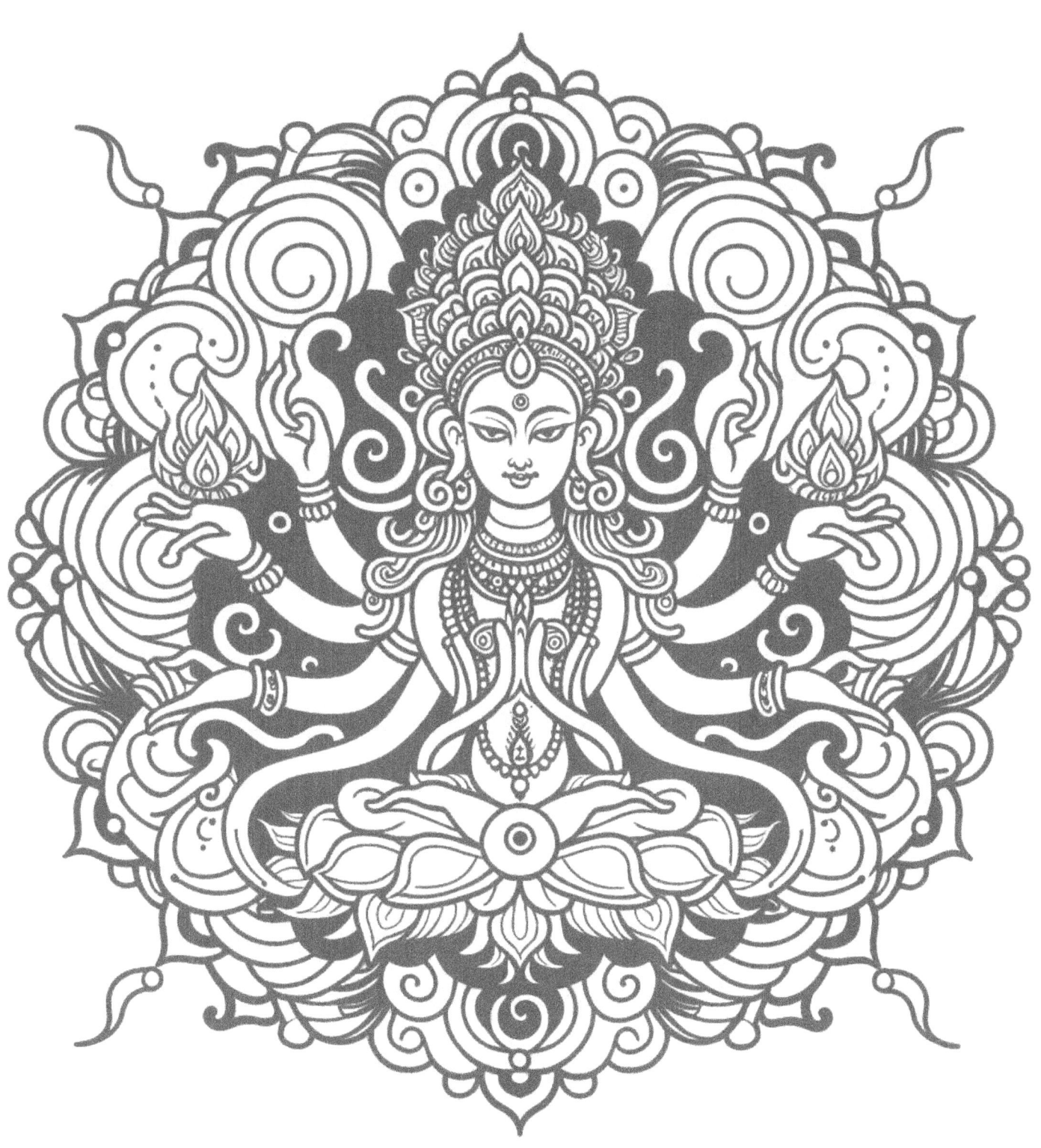

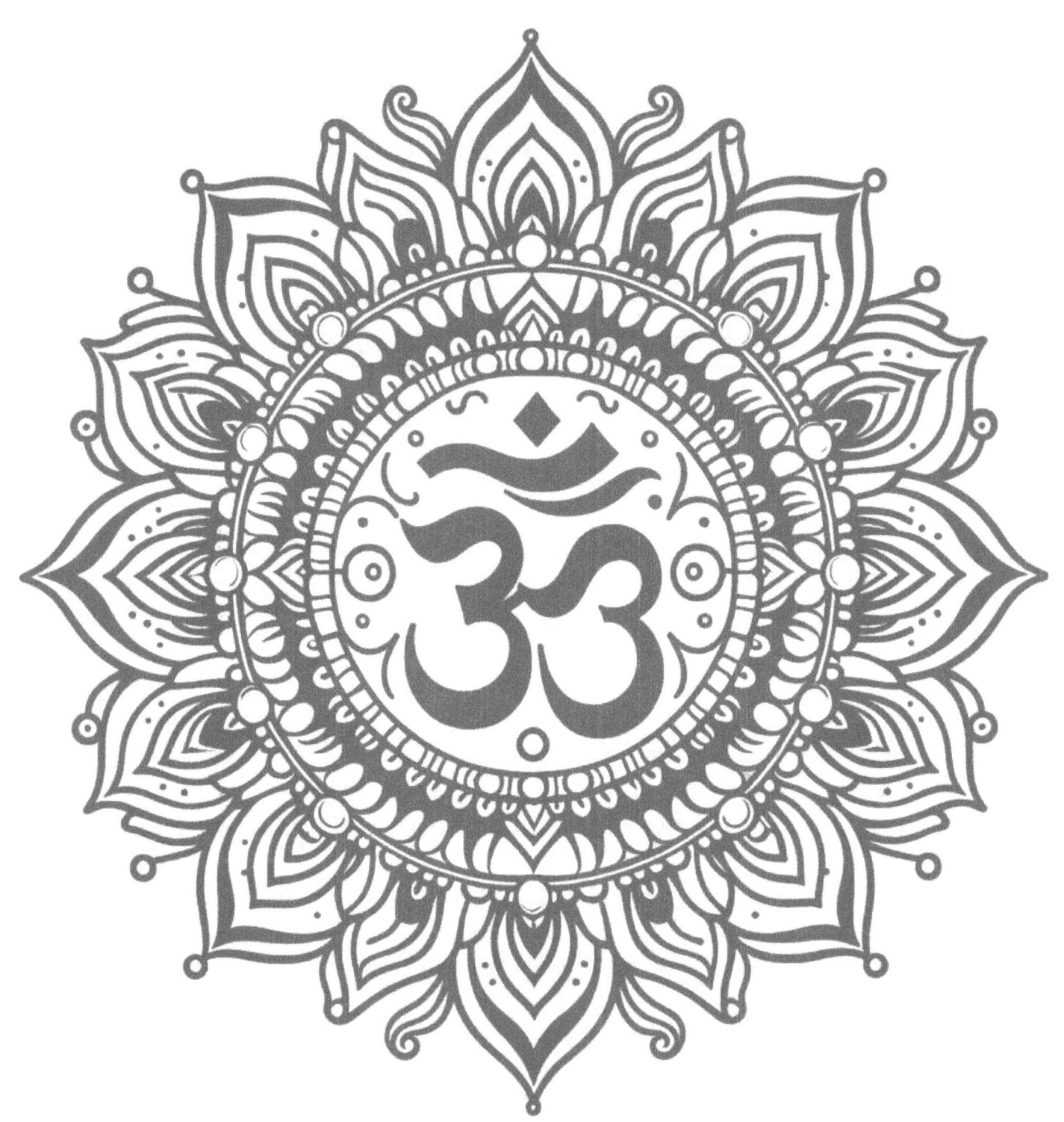